Beauty of
San Francisco

Beauty of
San Francisco

Text: Lee Foster
Concept & Design: Robert D. Shangle

First Printing September, 1990
Published by LTA Publishing Company
2735 S.E. Raymond Street, Portland, Oregon 97202
Robert D. Shangle, Publisher

"Learn about America in a beautiful way."

Library of Congress Cataloging-in-Publication Data

Foster, Lee, 1943-

    Beauty of San Francisco.

      1. San Francisco (Calif.) — Description — Views.

      2. San Francisco (Calif.) — Description — Guide-books.

I. Shangle, Robert D.   II. Title.

F869.S343F67   1989   979.4'61   89-12417

ISBN 0-917630-96-3

ISBN 0-917630-49-1 (pbk.)

Contents

Introduction

A Northern Californian of long standing will sometimes make a conversational reference to "the city." A non-Californian hearing this may wonder if the speaker means Sacramento, Oakland, Berkeley, Palo Alto, or some other place. But "the city" is unmistakably San Francisco. The code word and its connotations are immediately understood by a Northern Californian: San Francisco has no equal. Other towns may exceed it in limited ways; none can match it as a place where urban civilization and culture have achieved an exhilarating level of sophistication.

San Francisco is everybody's favorite city. Public opinion polls have indicated that San Francisco is one of the most visited United States cities, not only by Americans and their proximate neighbors, the Canadians, but by visitors from abroad such as the Japanese. Those who come here share a conviction that the good life flourishes in San Francisco, a premise that certainly holds true when the city's fine hotels, restaurants, and shops are taken into account. But the community's real assets are less easily identifiable in a specific way. They include, of course, its matchless physical setting and the manmade things, like the Golden Gate Bridge and the cable cars, which have become an integral part of that setting. But perhaps the city's most solid asset is something very immaterial — its atmosphere of personal freedom.

San Francisco is a city in love with its past, but may be excused such self-absorption. No other city in the United States has a past marked with such violent and legendary events as its beginnings during the Gold Rush and its (temporary) ending, the earthquake and fire of 1906.

San Francisco is sometimes saluted for its civilized traditions, but it also offers an ambience of choice, an opportunity for lifestyle exploration, architectural daring, culinary novelty — in short, the search for new answers in all areas of human activity.

— Lee Foster

Everybody's Favorite City

The taxi driver in Mazatlan asks where I'm from, and I reply, "San Francisco. " His face lights up, "Ah, what a beautiful city!" Then he confides that he hasn't been there, but somehow he knows. While conversing with a lady in Paris, I mention that I am from San Francisco, and she responds, "Now that's the American city I'd like to see." A friend in Minneapolis envies me for living here because, she says, "There's so much happening out there."

While most people espouse the merits of their familiar setting, it is surprising how many rank San Francisco as their next favorite place. The magnetism of these 47-square miles on the tip of a peninsula is astonishing. Each year some 3 plus million visitors pass through the city, making their care and feeding the largest local industry. Mobile young people, after finishing college, crowd in with the residents, creating keen competition for jobs in professional fields.

When then-mayor Joseph Alioto signed ordinance 307-09 on October 29, 1969, bestowing the title, "Official Song of the City and County of San Francisco" on *I Left My Heart in San Francisco*, while Tony Bennett crooned amidst a backdrop of cable cars, the mayor was acknowledging the satisfying fantasy that the song's lyrics project, even if their repetition sometimes seems cloying to a native. Cable cars, hills, fog, and bay are ingredients in the San Francisco recipe. The city has also inspired numerous other songs.

An obvious San Francisco trademark is, without doubt, the cable car, a charming and paradoxical conveyance. Cable cars appear improbable, yet they are an efficient means for carrying people up steep hills.

Other arrangements, requiring steel or rubber tires, would polish the surface of the street or rail until, with the assist of lubricating rains, the surface would be treacherous. The cable cars appear antiquated, but they are a favorite means of transportation for the visitor, an outing in themselves, and they are also the means of everyday travel of the San Franciscan. By comparison, what other city's mass transit system is enjoyed for the pleasure of the trip alone?

The Cable Car Barn and Museum, at Washington and Mason streets, presents the history of these charmers and, amazingly enough, lets you gaze closeup at the innards of the system, a 750-horsepower engine turning massive steel wheels and thick cables that can pull at one time a maximum of 31 cars, each weighing six tons, at a speed of $9^1/_2$ miles per hour, up a 21-percent grade. The 127 miles of track in the 1880s have been reduced to merely $10^1/_2$ miles today.

At the cable car turnaround on Powell, you can see Hallidie Plaza, named after this pioneer inventor. It's an appropriate place to board the 20th-century extension of his mass transit vision, the BART (Bay Area Rapid Transit).

When man has altered the environment of San Francisco, controversy has usually accompanied the result. However, there is near universal agreement on the merits of one creation, the Golden Gate Bridge, the most photographed work of man on the earth. In a society whose monuments are secular, the Golden Gate Bridge ranks high and has no peer among bridges. Completed in 1937 under the direction of engineer Joseph Strauss, the bridge is open to pedestrians and traffic. Painted international orange, a color that offsets favorably the coastal flora of Marin County hillsides to the north, the bridge spans a narrow waterway of powerful inrushing and outgoing tides where the Sacramento-San Joaquin River systems drain into the sea.

To the south extends the Bay Bridge, a grey $8^1/_4$-mile mass of steel that connects the East Bay with San Francisco. The Bay Bridge is longer and less glamorous than the Golden Gate, but more vital to the commercial life of the city.

San Francisco pleases partly because of its manageable size. In a short time you feel that you can know it, though not begin to exhaust it. Some cities sprawl, but San Francisco has a compact, easy-to-get-around-in feeling. The 40 hills always present a new vista, a varied, seldom-repeated appearance, aided by the changing light and fog. Cable cars, busses, and BART carry people efficiently to their destinations. With the longest street, Geary, measuring only five miles, San Francisco is one of America's best walking towns. Mountain climbers may find it interesting to know that the steepest streets are Filbert between Leavenworth and Hyde, and 22nd between Church and Vicksburg, both with a 31.5 percent gradient. Lombard, "the most crooked street in the world," between Leavenworth and Hyde, delights those who seek out the picturesque.

San Francisco offers natives and visitors an air of freedom, a chance to think what is unthinkable elsewhere and to live in ways declared outrageous in other parts of the country. San Francisco presents a holiday from conformity, a place to let down, an opportunity to be what you wish, perhaps also to glimpse behavioral arrangements whose time is yet to come.

To some extent this freedom developed because of the city's origin. During the Gold Rush people from all over the world poured in, forming an instant society. The diversity of backgrounds required a tolerance that was by no means complete, but was notable when compared with other societies. As a port town, San Francisco has always been open to influences from the Orient and elsewhere.

This openness has made the city a lifestyle laboratory, where people experiment with ways of living, with relating to each other and to the environment. Often these experiments set trends that become wide-spread elsewhere. For example, if the national environment movement could be said to have had a birth, perhaps the most significant single event was the 1962 rejection by San Franciscans of a freeway that would have cut people off from the waterfront between the Ferry building and the Golden Gate. You can still see this freeway literally hanging in the air where it was stopped along the Embarcadero.

San Francisco has always been a place of good living, with lively bars and superb restaurants. The variety of restaurants stuns the imagination. Have you ever eaten buffalo stew and scanned a decor of "flotsam-jetsam" western Americana? In every category of classic food there are restaurants where *haute cuisine* is a reality. And there are always newcomers who make San Francisco a place for culinary discoveries. Many San Franciscans dream of their own perfect restaurant, and go through life sampling the alternatives, refining the vision.

Hotels of the city have been legendary since 1876 when William Ralston built his white and gold Palace Hotel at Market and Montgomery. Financed with five million uninflated dollars that Ralston amassed as his share of silver in Virginia City, Nevada's famous Comstock Lode, the Palace boasted 800 rooms and a palm court carriage entrance. The hotel's splendor was shattered by the earthquake and fire of 1906, but was meticulously rebuilt with the palm court transformed into an elegant dining room, the garden court, which should be glimpsed today for its grandeur.

The City in Love With Its Past

No American city has a love affair with its past more intense than San Francisco's. This may be narcissism, but of a harmless sort. The San Franciscan loves his Victorian architecture and wants to show it to you just as an Amsterdammer appreciates his 17th-century canal houses. And the San Franciscan dwells on the instant and accidental founding of the city — the Gold Rush — the way an informed Mexico City resident, showing you through the Museum of Anthropology, will recall the capricious decision to found Tenochtitlan when a priest sighted an eagle with a snake in its claws.

Each of the eras of San Francisco history remains alive today, both as artifacts you can see and as legend to nourish the imagination, starting with the tranquility of the Spanish-Mexican era from 1776 to the 1840s, then the exhilarating shock of the Gold Rush after 1848, followed by the reflective gentility of the later 19th century, all shattered by the earthquake and fire of 1906.

The Spanish era of San Francisco's history can only be described as bucolic and, in some respects, idyllic. In 1776 Juan Bautista de Anza completed a long trek northward from San Ignacio de Tubac to establish, here, a presidio and settlement. Following close upon de Anza was the indefatigable Franciscan, Junipero Serra, who founded Mission San Francisco de Asis, his sixth in California. Popularly known as Mission Dolores, after a nearby swamp, the structure at 16th and Dolores still stands, restored but not altered, the oldest unchanged building in San Francisco. Constructed of sun-dried bricks, the walls are four feet thick. Since no nails were available, wooden pegs and rawhide held the building together. The lines of the mission suggest the simplicity and austerity of frontier California at a time when the Declaration of Independence preoccupied the 13 colonies on the east coast of the continent. Don Luis Antonio Arguello, the first Spanish governor of California, lies buried in the small adjacent graveyard. The interior roof remains as it was painted in angular shapes more than 150 years ago by Indians using vegetable dyes.

By the 1830s San Francisco and Monterey proved attractive to a few Yankees, who saw the area from whaling or trading ships and decided to settle here. Adventurers of other nationalities also stopped and stayed, among them entrepreneur John Sutter, who touched at San Francisco and then pushed inland to the area of Sacramento where he hoped to establish an agricultural empire.

The event that was to transform the drowsy, sand-duned trading post of San Francisco into an international city occurred at a sawmill that James Marshall was building in 1848 for John Sutter on the American River, about 110 air miles northeast of the city. Marshall discovered some yellow nuggets in the race below the mill. When it was determined that the material was indeed gold, the story could hardly be suppressed.

Between 1848 and 1852 California was transformed from a pastoral scattering of Spanish-Mexican villages with a population of 15,000 to a restless prospecting region of 250,000. Statehood came in 1850. By 1852 an estimated $200 million in gold had been mined.

In San Francisco you can see a brick fortification remaining from this era called Fort Point, immediately below the south anchor of the Golden Gate Bridge. Juan Bautista de Anza first planted a cross here in 1776 and the Spaniards erected a crude stockade by 1794. Today the Civil War era fort remains as a prime example of 19th-century United States military architecture. Fittingly, in the city dedicated to peaceful St. Francis, the fort never fired a shot in anger.

The Jackson Square Historic District, bounded by Kearney, Washington, Sansome, and Pacific streets, is an interesting cluster of brick buildings from the 1850s and 60s. The Hotaling Building at 451

14

Jackson was once a liquor warehouse. At the corner of Montgomery and Jackson streets stands the Lucas Turner & Co. Bank, begun in 1853 by William T. Sherman. Today lawyers, designers, art dealers, and antique dealers occupy the historic building in the city's core.

Each Jackson Square structure has its story to tell. The Langerman Building at 722 Montgomery, was built in 1849-50, then rebuilt after a fire. It served first as a tobacco warehouse, became the Melodeon Theater, later was an auctioneering site, and then a Turkish bath. The adjacent Genella Building tells more of the story of San Francisco's early diversity. Joseph Genella erected it in 1853-54 for his residence and business in china and glassware. Later activities included a bullion dealership, merchandise brokerage, a Spanish newspaper, and a mining office. Near the corner of Sansome and Clay the *Niantic*, a grounded ship, served as a hotel. Hundreds of abandoned hulls became floating residences and stores during the Gold Rush.

The Wells Fargo Bank History Room is another instructive stop. There you can view a Concord stagecoach and read the free giveaway, a copy of the 1887 *Tips For Stagecoach Drivers*. This small museum contains such monetary curiosities as a $50 octagonal gold slug issued by the United States assay office in 1852. Wells Fargo also tells the story of its antagonist Black Bart, the most prominent highway robber of 19th-century California. Bart robbed 28 stages single-handedly, never harming a passenger, leaving mocking doggerel verse at the scene of the crime.

While downtown, catch the California and then the Powell cable cars to Union Square, named after a mass meeting in 1861 when Californians decided to side with the Union. If there is one place in San Francisco where you can see the whole spectrum of humanity pass by, it is Union Square, so seat yourself on a bench for a restful hour in the sun to watch the kaleidoscopic procession of people.

After browsing the smart shops of the area, such as Gump's, with its remarkable collection of jade, catch the streetcar on Market to the Civic Center and peruse the large building of Italian Renaissance design,

City Hall. Walk through its regal interior and then browse the Public Library opposite. Behind City Hall lies the Opera House War Memorial, where the Museum of Modern Art sponsors changing shows.

San Francisco's circa 1860-1900 Victorian houses, whether palaces or modest residences, add much to the charm of the city. You can tour one of the most striking and best preserved of these dwellings, the Haas-Lilienthal House, 2007 Franklin, built in 1886. Its gables, bay windows, turret tower, and exuberance of gingerbread makes Haas-Lilienthal a classic Queen Anne, paralleled in its Victorian accoutrements only by the conservatory greenhouse in Golden Gate Park. The interior still houses much of the original decor, with mahogany walls, marble hearths, and fine tapestries.

The adjacent residential area, known as Pacific Heights, is considered one of San Francisco's choice living areas. Some other prominent Victorians are the Spreckles mansion and the California Historical Society building. The latter is open to visitors and is filled with period furnishings. Streets adjacent to Lafayette square offer many examples of Victorian architecture. At 1000 California stands the James Flood Mansion, built in 1886 by the Comstock-silver-lode millionaire. Today the flood Mansion is the last of the great meansions from the baronial days of the mining and railroad kings. Others in the neighborhood of the flood Mansion were destroyed by the fires that followed the earthquake.

The great earthquake and fire that destroyed San Francisco on April 18, 1906 has had a profound effect on the sensibility as well as physical look of the city. The shaking was not as devastating as the three days of fires, fed by broken natural gas lines and checked only with dynamite because the water mains were destroyed and private wells proved inadequate.

As a result of the earthquake, with 28,000 buildings and 500 people lost, San Francisco developed a fondness for firemen, whether expressed in Lillie Hitchcock Coit's fire nozzle or in Coit Tower (a splendid place to view the city).

San Francisco and the Golden Gate Bridge

The Coit Tower

Alcatraz Island

Golden Gate Park Conservatory

The Transamerica Building

San Francisco City Hall

San Francisco Skyline and The Bay Bridge from Treasure Island

San Francisco Skyline from Alamo Square

Fisherman's Wharf

Alcatraz Island

Palace of Fine Arts

Fisherman's Wharf

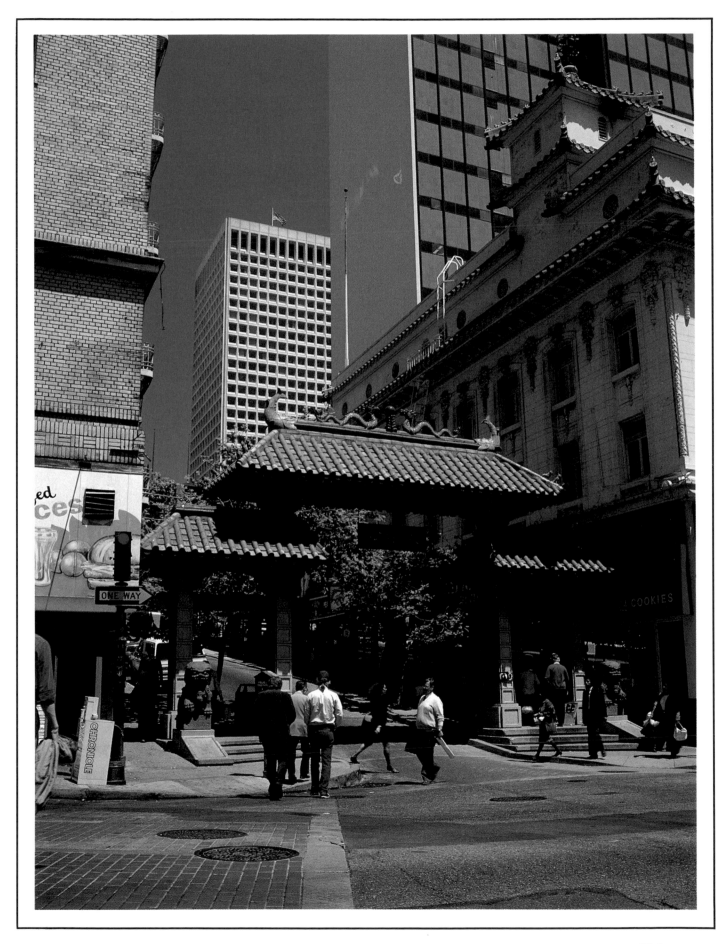

Chinatown

San Francisco at Sunrise

San Francisco at Sundown

Saints Peter and Paul Church

Above San Francisco

San Francisco Skyline from Marina Park

San Francisco from Treasure Island

Fisherman's Wharf

Above San Francisco

Entering San Francisco Bay

Aquatic Park and Telegraph Hill

At day's end, from the Oakland hills

Lombard, between Hyde and Leavenworth Streets

The Coit Tower from Russian Hill

Mission San Francisco de Asis (Mission Dolores)

The San Francisco Bay Area

Marina Park

Peace Pagoda in Japan Center

Fisherman's Wharf

Fishermans Wharf Entrance

Union Square

Japanese Garden, Golden Gate Park

Powell and Hyde Cablecar

Dutch Windmill, Golden Gate Park

Above Sausalito

Oakland

Beringer Brothers Winery, Napa Valley

Mission San Carlos Borromeo de Carmelo, Carmel

Point Bonita Lighthouse

Sonoma County Courthouse

Winchester House, San Jose

Rosicrucian Egyptian Museum, San José

Pigeon Point Lighthouse

Whaler's Cove, Point Lobos

Stanford University

Christian Brothers Winery, Napa Valley

The earthquake has always been viewed by San Franciscans with a *carpe diem* irreverence, partly because a repeat performance is inevitable. Lyrics of a song by Charles Field, referring to the Hotaling liquor warehouse in Jackson Square, caught the spirit of the city's response:

> "If, as they say, God spanked the town
>   for being over frisky,
> Why did He burn the churches down
>   and spare Hotaling's whiskey?"

The city's wharf area also leans heavily on the nostalgia aroused by its historic buildings. The two wharf complexes on Beach Street, Ghirardelli Square and the Cannery, are former factories that have acquired a patina of romance over the years. Domingo Ghirardelli's building was a Civil War uniform factory, a woolen works, and, eventually, a turn-of-the-century candy factory. Today it houses shops and restaurants, as does the Cannery, formerly the home of the Del Monte Fruit and Vegetable Cannery.

San Francisco's maritime history has been carefully preserved. At the foot of Hyde Street you can visit a park that is now a part of the National Maritime Museum. Maritime history comes alive on a Sunday in late May when the *Alma* leads a concourse of vintage sailing boats in a race around the Bay, called the Master Mariners Regatta. Each of the participants, ancient wooden sailing craft that were often working boats, receives its starting gun salute at the beach in front of the St. Francis Yacht Club. Today's race recalls the Master Mariners Regatta of the 1860s, when the competitive crews of lumber schooners and hay scows, after storing up their cabin fever for a year, would engage in a 4th of July race to determine once and for all who was the fastest.

Nature's Gift
to The City

San Francisco sits on the edge of a peninsula separating the Pacific Ocean from San Francisco Bay, one of the world's great natural harbors. With water on three sides, fog rolling in and out, and 40 hills to present the drama, the experience of San Francisco amounts to an unusual wedding of urban amenities and natural features. Of the city's hills Davidson is the highest and Twin Peaks, the geographic center, commands the most sweeping views.

On many mornings and evenings, especially in summer, a heavy blanket of fog pushes across the city, triggering a dazzling interplay of light and shadow. The cool damp air of the fog holds San Francisco's temperature at a comfortable mean of 57 degrees with only moderate variations. In a normal rainy season, 21 inches drop on the city between mid-November and mid-April. The westerly winds that propel sailboats around the bay on sunny afternoons also keep San Francisco relatively free of smog, even in the warmest month, which is September.

Even within the city, the appreciator of wild nature can find some satisfaction. Consider the Mycological Society, which gathers at 9 a.m. each Sunday morning in winter, near the Rodin fountain at the Palace of the Legion of Honor, and makes a foray into the wild Land's End area looking for mushrooms. The wild mushrooms in the area are prolific, nurtered by the wet fog and bright sun. Shaggy manes, *agaricus rodmanii*, parasols, and various *boletus* are all eagerly sought and gathered in great numbers by the mycophagists, or mushroom eaters, within the ranks. The poisonous *Amanitas pantherina* and *muscaria* are merely observed. Each November the Academy of Sciences in Golden Gate Park hosts a mushroom fair that displays hundreds of wild mushrooms from the San Francisco region. These autumn gatherings are lavish and colorful, both for mushrooms and their admirers.

Another species of nature lover, genus San Francisco, can be observed at the foot of Hyde Street, headquarters of the Dolphin Club, an association founded by a half dozen German sports enthusiasts in 1877. The Dolphins specialize in swimming the chilly bay waters. You can usually see them streaking across the cove in front of Aquatic Park. On more ambitious days they swim across the bay, itself, fighting not only the chill but the swift currents.

When looking at San Francisco today, it is difficult to imagine that in the 19th century much of the western half was a shifting sand dune that some expert landscapers, such as Frederick Law Olmsted, despaired of taming. Coastal strand plant communities in relatively undisturbed states can be found on the hillsides in the south part of Sutro Heights Park, on dunes around Baker Beach, and on hillsides between Lincoln Boulevard and the beach west of the Golden Gate. In the spring these areas show dozens of native wildflowers of every shape and color, including Indian paint brush, yellow sand verbena, California poppy, seaside daisy, wild buckwheat, beach lupine, yarrow, and yellow bush lupine.

Because so much of San Francisco, in 1868, was an uninhabited sand dune region, the city fathers showed some foresight when they set aside 800,000 uninflated dollars for the purchase and development of 1,017 acres to be known as Golden Gate Park. Like the great hotels and the opera house, the park was both a gesture to the future and a legacy, an index of the confidence that San Franciscans had in the city's growth and destiny, a sense that the city would later need the civilizing and recreational opportunities afforded by a major park.

The man who transformed Golden Gate Park, then about 730 acres of dunes and 270 acres of arable land scattered with live oaks, was a small, stocky Scotsman, born in Stirling in 1846, who migrated to California in 1870. In 1887 the park commission appointed John McLaren as park superintendent, a post he held for 59 years, until his death in 1943.

McLaren's first task was to continue his predecessors' efforts at anchoring the dunes with a mixture of ice plant, northern European beach grass, and the tea tree from Australia. One year he asked for and received from the park commission the street sweepings of San Francisco as his birthday present. With this ample supply of horse manure, he built the ground turf that allowed later impressive plantings of trees and meadows. McLaren, who liked to be addressed with the simple term, "boss gardener," planted more than 5,000 different kinds of shrubs, flowers, and trees in the park. He used the Monterey Cypress to good advantage at the west end where it thrives in the sea winds. In the quieter recesses of the park, he favored the Australian eucalyptus, with its dappled bark and heady gum smell. The climate was his ally in the rose garden, where roses bloom even in December.

Along Kennedy Drive, stop to admire the Victorian conservatory, a lacy glass confection covering hothouse begonias and tropical plants, with a greeting card of flowers on the front lawns.

You can relax over tea at the Japanese Tea Garden, especially enjoyable at April cherry blossom time. Nearby are the art holdings of the De Young Memorial Museum and the natural history displays of the California Academy of Sciences. At the Steinhardt Aquarium you can see a golden garibaldi fish that grows up to 14 inches off the California coast. Summer concerts in the music concourse are presented free on Sunday afternoons.

The famous Strybing Arboretum is almost a park within a park, with its acres of labeled trees and shrubs. Of special interest is the California native plant section.

You will look in vain for a "Keep Off The Grass" sign. John McLaren stressed that the park should be used, including its 11 lakes, 2 stadiums, 27 miles of footpaths, and 16 miles of bridle paths.

The nature lover in San Francisco also owes a thank you for the inadvertent preservation occasioned by the presence of the United States Army, whose 1,400-acre Presidio, largest military post in a United States city, now gives San Francisco a huge green breathing space and playground.

As if to augment John McLaren's dream, the parks of San Francisco are expanding rather than contracting. Indeed, the appreciation of nature and a deliberate effort to arrest any encroachment on nature characterizes the people of Marin County and San Francisco. The newest development is the creation of a 34,000-acre Golden Gate National Recreation Area to embrace the many parklands in the immediate San Francisco-and-north region. Starting at the southwest end of San Francisco, this park wraps a 10-mile ribbon of greenery and sand around the western and northern shores of the city.

Beginning at the southwest are the Fort Funston dunes, fortunately held by the military until they had no more strategic value and the public had the will and resources to acquire them. Hang-gliding enthusiasts favor Funston as the best west coast site for catching the winds that blow landward, bounce off the cliffs, and shoot up, carrying hang gliders aloft for minutes or hours as the pilot chooses, drifting up and down the beaches, confident that in any emergency a gentle landing could be made on the sand and iceplant terrain.

Stretching northward is the long Ocean Beach. At the end stands jutting rocks, home for cormorants and barking sea lions, though misnamed Seal Rock. Between Land's End and the bridge is Baker Beach, another fine stretch for surf fishing, strolling, wading, and hiking. Picnickers favor protected places in the adjacent cypress forests.

The most recently added attraction for nature lovers in San Francisco is the Golden Gate Promenade, a 3$^{1}/_{2}$-mile stretch of beach between Fisherman's Wharf and the Golden Gate. As this area becomes cleared and landscaped in future years, it will emerge as one of the great urban walks in the world. More of a hike than a promenade, the path gives you a good sense of the bay, beach, islands, and sailboats. Beachcombers delight in the debris that the sea turns up here. To make this walk, begin with the promenade signs at the wharf or at Marina Green.

The promenade offers your best opportunity in the city to see the bird life that thrives on and around San Francisco Bay. Cormorants are abundant during the spring and can be seen diving for small fish. Terns also dive from the air and grab their prey while scarcely losing a wingbeat. Occasionally brown pelicans can be seen skimming over the waters only a few inches above the waves. Blackbirds, killdeer, and sanderlings are abundant along the walk.

San Francisco is one of the few cities whose outlying parts are accessible only by boat. Alcatraz Island has some natural features of note, but larger Angel Island, reached by ferryboat from Pier 43, offers more for the nature enthusiast. On Angel Island you can see a wide range of California native plants while walking, picnicking, or bicycling. This greenery is, like the Presidio, an unplanned gift from the military. At times past Angel Island served as a kitchen garden for the Alcatraz prison, a backup area for our soldiers in wartime, and an immigration station. In the 1970s Angel Island was also an example of nature gone askew when the balance was upset by the exclusion of predators. The deer population exploded and depleted the vegetation until park authorities took steps to thin the herd to manageable numbers. Today Angel Island approximates the natural setting that Juan Manuel de Ayala saw when he sailed the first boat through the Golden Gate in 1775.

The City of Unmeltable Ethnics

A "hyphenated" American has never had to apologize for his ethnicity in San Francisco, the city composed of ethnics. Though it has become popular in the last decade throughout the country to embrace one's national origins, it has always been the custom to do so in San Francisco. Those without an ethnic specialty in San Francisco often tend to follow one of the lifestyle innovations that differentiate in a manner more radical than ethnic.

San Francisco's Chinatown, largest Chinese community outside the orient, began in the 1850s when Chinese fled natural disaster and political upheaval in the south China Kwangtung Province and city of Canton. Today about one in ten San Franciscans is of Chinese origin. In the 1860s and 70s thousands of Chinese workers came to construct the Central Pacific Railroad. In the past decade Chinatown has been rejuvenated by 40,000 immigrants from Hong Kong and Taiwan, filling a gap left when Chinese moved out of the city or to some other area. The opening up of trade with mainland China in recent years has also brought renewed vitality to Chinatown.

Portsmouth Square is the focus for the visitor and for the Chinese living in the immediate area. In the early morning tai chi chuan practitioners do exercises there. Later in the day children and older adults enjoy the sun in the park, feed the pigeons, and play Chinese chess. To know Chinatown you must walk it, beginning with Portsmouth Square, once the focus of San Francisco when the Bay waterline came nearly to the area. Here California pioneer Sam Brannan made an historic announcement that gold had been discovered, showing skeptics a few nuggets, which promptly turned San Francisco into a ghost town.

In 1880 Scottish writer Robert Louis Stevenson mused away his time here, just as hundreds of San Franciscans do every day. A stone bridge links Portsmouth Square with the Chinese Culture Foundation. The foundation sponsors interpretive exhibits about Chinese life in America. Other displays can be seen at the Chinese Historical Museum.

The food markets, especially on Stockton between Washington and Broadway, exhibit an awesome variety of Chinese vegetables, such as bok choi and chard, meat or fowl, including ducks and pigeons. The numerous fat ducks hanging raw or cooked and the bags of paper-thin dried fish are two unusual sights for the occidental, but on Stockton you may even see a butcher carve up a turtle.

Chinatown has many special places to browse, among them Old Chinatown Lane, which contains some of the few buildings in the area that survived the fires after the 1906 earthquake. The lane was noted for its proliferation of gambling and opium establishments. The Mandarin Co., 64 Wentworth, carried records, cassettes, and the original instruments used to create Chinese music. Three temples on Waverly Place are open for the mediator who seeks a quiet respite from the city. High quality jade and ivory carvings can be examined at Chinese Arts and Crafts and Jade Empire. The Mow Lee grocery, in business since 1856, is the oldest grocery in Chinatown.

Chinese New Year is a festive time for all San Franciscans. Firecrackers, a Chinese invention, turn the metal and stone canyons of the city into a deafening battleground. Children of all ages wait along the parade route for a glimpse of the huge dragon of the Chinese New Year Parade, a lavish event.

With recent mayors bearing the names Moscone and Alioto, it should be no surprise that San Francisco has a substantial Italian colony, residents of Italian descent, focussed historically in the North Beach area but now diffused throughout the city. In October the Italians celebrate

Columbus' discovery of America with a re-enactment of the event, a Columbus Day Parade, and the blessing of the fleet at Fisherman's Wharf. At the Aquatic Park courts, Van Ness and North Point, you can sometimes see bocce ball played. San Francisco is one of the few cities in the United States where Italians continue this lawn bowling tradition, said to have begun with the Romans in the time of the Caesars.

The Mexican-Americans of the Mission Districts have a startling new art form to show visitors, the wall mural, reminiscent of what a traveler might see in the works of Diego Rivera or Clement Orozco in Mexico. At the Mexican Museum, take in the current show and pick up a free walking map of the murals, four of which are especially prominent. They are located at the minipark on 24th, a half block east of Bryant, at 2922 Mission, at the BART station on 24th and Mission, and at 24th and Van Ness. These murals take as their theme the cycle of life, fertility, farming, Latin America, and the struggle of work. A fifth mural with an entirely different style and theme is the Mike Rios' cartoon creation about people and their legal problems, on the San Francisco Legal Assistance Building, 23rd and Folsom.

The main Mexican-American celebrations in San Francisco are Cinco de Mayo, recalling every May 5th the 1862 victory over the French at the Battle of Puebla; and the 16th of September, Mexican Independence Day, a week of parades, dances, and special festivities, including at City Hall the famous "El Grito de Dolores," a re-enactment of Miguel Hidalgo's historic yell announcing independence from Spain in 1810.

During the Cherry Blossom Festival, you can listen to Japanese folk songs, watch dancing, even hear the thunderous taiko (Japanese drum) concerts. On hand are masters of the various Japanese martial arts of judo, akido, kendo, kempo, taido, and karate. Displays present Japanese art, calligraphy, silk screens, bonsai, pottery, flower arranging, classical koto music, and the tea ceremony.

The Irish of San Francisco celebrate St. Patrick's Day on March 17 with all other nationals prepared to switch ethnic allegiance for the moment. Many San Franciscans take up the offer. With so many pubs bearing names such as Harrington's, O'Keefe's, and McGowan's, there's plenty of free corned beef and cabbage, plus green beer and stirring Irish folk music. The St. Patrick's Day Parade draws participants as diverse as the Irish Wolfhounds of Sebastopol and the Twirl Girls of San Bruno. Like other ethnic groups, the Irish have their grand Ball and Miss Shamrock.

As an index of the city's internationalism, consider that some 22 foreign language papers are produced in the San Francisco area. It has been argued that the proceedings of the United Nations would have been more fruitful if that organization could have stayed in San Francisco after its founding here in 1945.

The City of Innovation

San Francisco has always been a city that encouraged innovation in personal living, institutions, and architecture. When the innovation worked well, it quickly became a tradition. But the tradition was never seen as sacred. There was always room for the next innovator.

Take the Farmer's Market, at 100 Alemany, as an example. In 1943 the gas and sugar shortages of World War II forced Bay Area canneries to cancel their pear contracts, so farmers brought their produce to San Francisco to sell it directly to the people. Apples, then vegetables, followed pears. Today the tradition persists, with 40-plus farmers from 40-plus California counties bringing some 80-plus commodities to this market without benefit of a middleman. The annual Spring Daffodil Festival in April on Maiden Lane, near Union Square, is another such tradition, an urban delight that caught on and was repeated.

There was a time when the best views of San Francisco were limited to three choices: the Top of the Mark, in the Mark Hopkins Hotel; the Crown Room, in the Fairmont Hotel; and the Starlight Roof at the Sir Francis Drake Hotel. But then came the new downtown structures and their superlative platforms. The Carnelian Room of the Bank of America places you 52 stories above the town. Among the other options, the Hyatt Regency's Equinox Room revolves, making a complete circle every 43 minutes.

San Francisco has always been a good place to listen to music. Through capable promotors, such as Bill Graham, San Francisco in the 1960s and 70s became a launching ground for hundreds of new rock groups. But that didn't mean the city abandoned its symphony. Edo de Waart, a Dutch conducter of the Rotterdam Philharmonic who contracted to conduct the San Francisco Symphony in the early 1980s, remarked, "The breadth of community support for the symphony in San Francisco impresses me. In Rotterdam we have a more stratified Friends of the Orchestra. But in San Francisco interest in symphony with all the committees spreads much more widely throughout the community."

To some extent the city, itself, has always been regarded as a work of art. The controversial innovation in the last decade has occurred in the downtown area of the 51-acre Golden Gateway development, west of Battery Street. These new buildings and their immediate surroundings are worth a walk, beginning at the Transamerica Pyramid at Washington and Montgomery. The scale and daring of such buildings pleases some San Franciscans and disturbs others ("The Transamerica Pyramid would be okay if they'd just take it down after Christmas.") A redwood grove planted next to the Pyramid has won wide acclaim as a brilliant spot of greenery amidst the stone, glass, and concrete.

San Francisco has always been in the forefront of lifestyle innovations. A milieu of personal freedom has been created through a mixture of tolerance and the anonymity of an urban area. One celebrated example of what is now woven into the city's history is the saga of Emperor Norton. If there ever was a San Franciscan marching to a different drummer, it was Joshua Norton. He was an Englishman, who came to San Francisco in 1849 at age 30 with $40,000 at his command, plus the skills required to parlay this sum into a quarter-million dollar fortune. At this point in his career, Norton learned that his reach exceeded his grasp. While attempting to corner the rice market, he gambled everything and lost. Then Norton went into seclusion, emerging finally from his dark night of introspection a changed man, at least from his own perspective. He now believed he was Emperor Norton I. Fortunately, he had friends, was declared harmless, and was quickly raised to the status of city buffoon. As the emperor he wore an ornate military uniform, complete with sword, and marched about the city, faithfully attended by a retinue of his two favorite dogs,

Bummer and Lazarus. He was allowed to "command" dinners gratis at local restaurants and to write small checks that the local banks honored in support of municipal comedy. Periodically he read proclamations re-affirming that he was indeed Emperor Norton I of the United States and Protector of Mexico. On occasion his proclamations ordered the dissolution of the Republican and Democratic parties in the interest of peace. When he died in 1880, the city gave him a sumptuous funeral.

To some degree Emperor Norton lives in the 20th century in all the unusual lifestyles that San Francisco nourishes. The city is the center of the spiritual self-help and growth disciplines. Est, Arica, Silva Mind Control, Transcendental Meditation, Zen Buddhism, Rolfing, and Bio-energetics are but a few of the systems offered to the spiritual explorer.

Steeped in history, yet modern and bustling, San Francisco is a city of constantly changing moods, sights, sounds and faces. Immortalized in song and story, cosmopolitan, breathtakingly beautiful, and always exciting, San Francisco is truly "everybody's city."